Strength for Today
Hope for Tomorrow

MILO MLANGENI

Strength for Today
Hope for Tomorrow

INSPiRED
PUBLISHING

Strength for Today, Hope for Tomorrow
First Edition, First Impression 2020
ISBN 978-1-990961-31-1
Copyright © Milo Mlangeni
Published by:
Inspired Publishing
PO Box 82058 | Southdale | 2135
Johannesburg, South Africa
Email: info@inspiredpublishing.co.za

CONTENTS

- DEDICATION -

I dedicate this book to my son, Lungelo. In my lowest when
I did not have much hope, you were my main source of
inspiration. I found a reason to become a better person, to
weather whatever storms of life I came across and to keep
pressing on because of you. May you grow to be the lover of
God that you already are.

Forever in love,

Mom

- ACKNOWLEDGEMENTS -

My abounding gratitude goes to God, the wonderful Father of Grace. If not for His eternal mercy, I would not be who I am today. I am grateful for the gift to write, and for His guidance on what I should prepare as a message for all those who will have an opportunity to read this book. All my life He has been faithful, to Him be the glory.

I would like to send my heartfelt thanks to all the people who have played a role in making this dream come true:

My family, who are always supportive to me no matter what venture I undertake. Mom, you are forever my pillar, your prayers and continuous encouragement have played a huge role in who I am today. My brother, keep the light shining, we are following in the path that you are continuously lighting up. My sister, Nontukuso Ndira, words fail me. I am amazed at how you always believe in my dreams, and you always see the best in me. Thank you for your continuous support.

All my friends, women of prayer and brethren that surround my life. If I were to mention you all by name my ink would run dry, but you know yourselves. Allow me to say I appreciate your presence in my life. God has allowed you in my life so you could make an impact in my realising this dream.

To all my spiritual mentors and every servant of God I have served under, I will forever be grateful to you. I send a special word of gratitude to my Pastors Chuks and Augusta Ozabor. Your teachings have practically restored my faith, inspired and transformed me from one level of glory to the other. I thank God for granting me an opportunity to be under your leadership and ministry. May God richly bless you.

To the Inspired Publishing team, you are simply the best! I feel supported and inspired by your enthusiastic guidance and coaching, this dream would not be a reality if it was not for you. You are truly an epitome of excellence in all you do. Thank you for being great cheerleaders!

- INTRODUCTION -

Whether prepared or not, the path of life brings every human being to the point of brokenness. This season of your life, no matter who seems to be around you, and how many they are, you will always face it alone. This is the point when you call on God, and He seems very far. You face separation and coldness, and you face hopelessness. A difficult question lingers in the back of your mind, "does God love me?"

If this is where you are right now, you are not alone. Many have been here before you, many are there, and many are still to be there. This is a place where hope and dreams can be exchanged for a destitute and overwhelming sense of loss. Dreams can be left, and life would be unbearable. Where there is no hope, there is no light. Where there is no light, there is no reason for the future. This is the time where you need to have an assurance that you are never forsaken. No matter how 'absent' God may seem, He is not away. When your senses don't feel Him, even there He is.

'Where can I go from Your Spirit? Or where can I flee from Your presence? If I ascend into heaven, You are there; If I make my bed in [c]hell, behold, You are there. If I take the wings of the morning, and dwell in the uttermost parts of the sea, even there Your hand shall lead me, And Your right hand shall hold me' Psalms 139:7-10 (NIV).

****

This book is meant to lighten your spirit and to assure you that whatever you are going through, things will get better. I pray that this book is a blessing to you and uplift your soul.

-ONE-

Grace that Abounds

It is a given to believe that we are saved by grace and that His grace is sufficient for us. It is easy for a believer to embrace that God's love is sufficient for him, and that love is not based on any good works a person has done, it is purely undeserved mercy. That comes easily when you have a strong relationship with God. When you maintain prayer times, worship and scripture reading the zeal for God stays alive, and you live a life of gratitude and appreciation of salvation and the love of God.

But, what happens when tough times come? What happens when the worst happens in your life, when you experience such gruesome storms and challenges that the core of your faith is tested? When you experience such trials that you never thought a Christian could experience? These are times when you can easily feel that God has let you down; the foundations of your faith and trust in God's love are tested.

When you have lived years of faith, keeping the word, tithing, serving in God's house, then all of a sudden your life takes a sharp turn, you face such experiences that even non-believers have not experienced, in such times your trust is being tested.

Loss is not the same.

You can lose material possessions and still firmly keep your trust in God.

You can lose relationships and perhaps loved ones and still hold on to trust and faith. How do you hold up when over and above the physical, you lose your dreams, when you cannot see light or hope in your future? What happens when you feel empty inside and so dry, when the melody in your heart stops? What happens when you lose any sense of hope and direction, you lose the sense of worth and purpose?

What happens when you cannot tithe anymore? When you no longer feel the connection and your zeal to pray? Actually when you are questioning God, and you wonder if He does love you after all? What happens when the ground has shifted, you are no longer able to be that Christian you have always been. You wonder what happened to your years of serving God, at this moment you are cornered such that there is nothing you can do to change your present experience. You now begin to expect even the worse to happen, as you are not able to do anything you believed was the basis of your progress in life. You kept the tithe because you believe in it, now you cannot tithe; you basically wait to lose even the little that is left in your life as you are no longer able to keep your part of the covenant. Prayer sustained you and kept you over waters, now you cannot even complete a minute in prayer, so you know that you are spiritually doomed?

Then in the midst of all the turmoil, losses, struggle and failure, you realise this:

You never go to bed hungry, your basic needs are met. Amazingly you are able to get by, and your cupboards are not running dry. Just when you get to a point where you have used up all you have, provision comes from unexpected sources.

That is when you realise the meaning of grace.

As a Christian, when you are at a point of not even being able to finish the Lord's prayer, when you can't give or tithe, when worship no longer means anything to you,

God still hears

a whisper of need from your heart and provides for you. He still drops you a miracle here and there so that you never really go hungry; he still protects you from physical danger every day; that is when you learn the meaning of grace.

Finally, you get it, that grace is truly unmerited favour. We begin Christianity by grace, but along the way, we shift and believe that we get all the blessings because of our works.

Losing all the ability to actually provide your works, you realise that indeed God's grace abounds.

We always know about grace, but subconsciously we may think we are good Christians and God is pleased with our conduct, that is why we are receiving what we are receiving in life. But, the space of being at a loose end schools you that your actions do not earn you grace.

Whether in your eyes, you are the best or worst Christian, His response and love are still the same. Because of this grace, no matter how wrong your life has turned, you are still His child. No matter how far you feel from God, remain in this grace. This is the grace that carries you when life has stopped making sense. When the ground you stand on has shifted. When all your abilities are bitten down, this grace is the only anchor that keeps you standing; this is when you truly appreciate that,

'it is by grace you have been saved'.

A cry of supplication in time of despair

The world feels like a huge sea,
One is just swimming against waves endlessly
I do not want to be without faith
But my faith is challenged daily
Where is my God...? Sometimes that is what I think
But I remember that He said
He will never leave me nor forsake me.
Lord let not my troubles last too long
Let not my life end up in despair
Lord let not your servant reach a state of hopelessness,
Remember all your maidservants' supplications.
If the Lord cannot comfort me, then I
Have no comforter in this life
If God cannot come through for me
Then I have no hope in this life
I am blown like a paper blown by a wind,
With no direction and no vindication
But if my God be the God of Abraham,
Isaac and Jacob
The God of the living and the dead
The God of the bible, then my hope is not in vain

Only Lord, please, do not allow me
To sorrow to the point of despair
Please, Lord, it has been long!
Come through for me as before
In thee, I put my trust.
If you do not come through for me, I am doomed,
And I am a laughing stock to the world
With you, I believe I will be restored and made whole,
In thee, I put my trust.

Lifted Up By Grace:
Real Life Testimony

I had fully comprehended the term 'grace', since my becoming a Christian, or so I thought. I had it all together, my prayer life was kind of intact, I observed the basic Christian principles, I was committed to the local church, and my walk (in my eyes) was good before the Lord. Whenever I prayed, I had a clear conscience even to say 'Lord, I've walked well before you'. I withstood during the trying times and prevailed.

Unfortunately, I came to a point where my journey had a sharp turn. I got hard-pressed every side, things I never fathomed were possible to befall committed Christians did happen, and not just for a month or a year. I faced a long period of struggle, and unconsciously I began to lose everything. I lost my fervency; prayer life became non-existent, I couldn't lift even a finger in the house of the Lord. I lost all faith, except that I still believed there was God and that Christ died for me. I couldn't tithe or give. I felt so out of space and became convinced that God did not care anymore.

Nevertheless, I saw His Unmistaken Divine interventions. He provided, He led my path, He opened doors. I could not pray, but I saw answers. When I thought of throwing in the towel, He came through and refreshed my soul. Oh, what love I felt; finally, I fully comprehended the concept of grace. 'By grace, ye have been saved'.

'For it is by grace you have been saved, through faith—
and this is not from yourselves, it is the gift of God
—' Ephesians 2:8 (NIV).

I understood that even when I was already born again, my constant walk with Him and everything else I could do was only through the grace of God. The ability to do his will and to please Him only came from Him. The ability to stand, and having done all to keep standing only came from Him.

I want to encourage any person who may go through the darkest moments of their lives; God still has His eyes on you. It may not seem so, but one day you will know it. You will look back and see that He has been holding your hand all along. The sun will shine again, and after hard storms, you'll be able to appreciate His grace even more.

May His grace carry you

Start all over again

We started off with nothing, but us.
When we lose everything, as long as we do not lose ourselves,
we can start all over again.
In life, loss is real. We lose loved ones,
we lose jobs, we lose possessions,
at times to the point of being left with nothing but ourselves.
Be the person who is not afraid to start up again,
no matter what you have lost.
You may feel you lost the best in life, but God is able to restore
and enable you to have much more
and better than all you have lost.

TWO

The Bittersweet Power of Pain

Without struggle, I would not appreciate victory I wouldn't fully comprehend the joy of success if I had not failed If I have not lacked in my life, I would not celebrate provision If I had not been through storms, I wouldn't know how to dance in the rain

Without battles, I would not know my inner strength Through weaknesses, I discovered my capabilities My inner treasures were unearthed in times of adversity

It is in conflict that my character was tested

It is in my shame that His grace became evident It is in darkness that I learned the power of light

It is through our lowest that we discover our true strength Through adversity, we learn to appreciate the smallest things in life that others take for granted

In our worst times, we become our best, if we allow such times to build us instead of breaking us So indeed I thank God for both the valleys and for the mountain tops For sunrise and sunsets

It all continues to work for my/your good, always.

'What then shall we say to these things? If God is for us who can be against us?'
Romans 8:31 (NKJV).

Pain has a twist in the end, in that everything that has life is born in pain. If you look through history, you realise that every person who touched lives and changed history had gone through some pain. The bible says:

'But he knows the way that I take; when he has tested me, I will come forth as gold.'
Job 23:10 (NIV).

Gold has to go through purification of fire, in order to be what it is and have the kind of value we appreciate. God is very much aware of our pain, but He allows it because He knows we will make it through the pain. He also knows the end product. I agree that life has been painful, but I also know that the best of you is being birthed out of your pain.

There are qualities in you that you will only know about when facing certain circumstances.

When you face situations that force you to make decisions you have never faced, to fight battles, you have never fought, and to be on your own throughout. These circumstances push you to a point where you discover a strength that you never knew you possessed. You are pushed to stand your ground, to speak your voice, to be bold and to think on your feet. After harsh conditions you will discover that you are more resourceful, you have a story to share and your life is no longer about you alone, the story of your life becomes an encouragement to many.

In reality, no one listens to someone without a past. Few people, if any, can be inspired by someone who has had a perfect life. There is literally nothing people can learn from a life that has had no challenges. Everyone we look up to right now, everyone we are willing to sit down and take notes from, has certain experiences and hardships that we are able to learn from and apply as lessons in our own lives. So yes, your pain is not in vain and is not only about you. It will strengthen many. Jesus said to Peter:

> *'but I have prayed for you, that your faith may not fail; and you, when once you have turned again, strengthen your brothers'*
> *Luke 22:32 (NAS).*

The epitome of your beauty is in the midst of the scars. When all grief and sorrow is evident, it is when you raise your head to say:

'My beauty is beyond my scars. I am beautiful because I am the image of God, because I am the best of creation, because I am no one's copy, because I am a gem waiting to be explored. The scars meant to hide me became tools to dig in me to reveal the powerful diamond lying within me. To see my beauty, you have to go beyond my scars. Even if you do not, it does not stop me from reaching deep within and unleash what the world is yet to see'.

Images

Unveiling of Victors

The crux of your life is in the crushing
and the hard pressing of your life.
At the point of pouring
where you are buried and left to be dead,
that is where you reach a crescendo of the birth of a hero
that is unstoppable, unshakeable; that only has eyes
set on the price and walking towards the mark.
That is when you shed fears, doubts, uncertainties;
where you pull off the top layers
of neediness, dependency
and secondary citizenship.
It is where you get to the inner core layer of your being
that was created to reflect your maker,
the layer that is feisty,
swift, unbendable, unstoppable, brave, determined
and ready to conquer and occupy
her God given space that only she can fill.
When you open your eyes to this inner core, you realise that your
pouring, pain and ultimately 'seeming' death was a divine plan
to birth what is that will carry grace to fulfil the purpose of God.

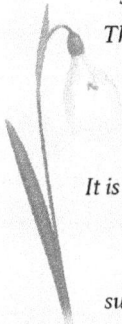

Engulfed and sinking
The testimony of 'Mary' following her divorce:

I feel like I have been engulfed by many waters; I am sinking deeper and deeper in the miry clay. Sheol has opened its wide mouth; loom and darkness want to swallow me. I run hard but only in my mind, I have no strength to even lift my head up. I am carrying a load of burden, and daylights have been turned off. This is the thickest night I have ever seen in my life; it seems like even the ground has been moved from be- neath my feet. I have no standing ground, I can't see ahead, on sides or behind. I am afraid to stretch my hand; every time I try to stretch it the worst happens. Am I falling deeper and deeper into a bottomless pit? Can somebody stop the process? Because I can't. I'm so helpless. God, maybe – where is God? Even within me, I can't find Him – how can I hope to reach the heavens?

This is meant to be my burial; this is meant to be my doom. A perfect design by a master enemy, who already have declared 'THE END'. No wonder the last thing he destroyed was my faith. What is a man without hope, when he doesn't even believe in prayer? The thoughts are playing in my head. I now believe it's the end.

I whisper a thought meant to be delivered to God if possible. I say all my trust is gone, my faith is gone, I'm finished. Somehow it does get delivered. I don't know how because I don't know the procedures of mail delivery in heaven, they are a mystery. At this point, I know I've lost everything when even faith is gone. But God! The ancient of days' steps in. He does not bring thunder or lightning; He does not bring earthquake, storm or hale. He brings a flicker of hope overnight, after the thought was delivered to Him. He puts me in a place where His word brings a flicker of hope.

Now I know this is enough with Him, just a flicker. It is a small beginning to a great unstoppable fire. The pit is still swallowing me, worst upon worst is happening. I don't have direction for my life. A voice says 'forget it, it's over'. But, I begin to rise, the flicker becomes a candle, then becomes a fire. I am rising out of the pit, out of the miry clay. Sheol loses its strength. God's word keeps coming. I now can pray, even if it's a couple of minutes. My faith rises. The giant wakes up;

I thought he was dead – but no, the giant in me was just sleeping. He wakes up, the warrior in me wakes up! I am beginning to feel ground under my feet. What was meant to kill me, God is turning it around, hallelujah!

'For by You I can run against a troop, by my God I can leap over a wall.'
Psalm 18:29 (NKJV).

- THREE -

Can You Trust God?

'Now faith is a substance of things hoped for, the evidence
of things not seen.'
Hebrews 11:1 (NKJV).

Faith is a pre-requisite for any prayer. One cannot come to God and receive anything without faith. The size of faith does not hinder God to answer us, because even when faith is little, so long as it is there, God answers.

'.... if you have faith as a mustard seed, you will say to this mountain, "Move from here to there", and it will move; and nothing will be impossible to you.' Matthew 17:20 (NKJV).

Most believers do have faith, no matter how little it is. The fact that one prays, goes to church and join in with other saints in prayer and fasting, that indicates a level of faith that God will answer.

Question is, do you trust God? after making your request known to him, do you trust that He is taking care of the matter? In a period between praying and receiving an answer, is your heart and mind at rest; knowing that He has your best interest? Many have faith, but trust remains an issue. Faith and trust go hand in hand. You cannot trust God when you do not believe in His supreme love.

Trust means that after you have prayed hard when instead of matters getting better, they get worse, you still trust Him. You trust that because you have prayed, He has all things under control. Trust relieves you from taking matters into your hands. It relieves you from sleepless nights and anxiety. When you trust God, after rebuking the storm by faith, you lie down trusting that as He has said in His word, so shall it be.

'Trust in the Lord with all your heart, and Lean not on
your own understanding'
Proverbs 3:5 (NKJV).

Some challenges do not require laying on of hands. You may go to all alter calls and come back with the same challenge. Those need you to trust the journey. While using faith, you need to trust that you have to walk the journey you are in, and God is with you. You need to trust that

He loves you too much to let you die in the wilderness,

therefore even when things don't make sense, you will get to the other side.

When there is no immediate provision – trust. When there is no immediate answer or solution – trust God. When you are cornered, and all hope is gone, when there is nothing to hold on to, the question is, can you trust Him? Can you trust that He loves you enough not to let you be destroyed? Trust works with your faith. Trust says

'Though He slay me, yet will I trust Him.'
Job 13:15 (NKJV).

Though the ground is removed, everything that was working for you is lost, the foundations of your life are shaken, what gave meaning to your life is slipping away. Trust will keep you hanging in there, and it will fuel your faith. When everything does not make sense, to the point of disappointment upon disappointment; your trust in God will keep you going.

When declarations seem not to be producing results; things get worse instead of better, your trust in God keeps you standing.

You cannot trust God if you do not believe that He loves you unconditionally and that He seeks what is best for your life.

You are loved by God. He paid the highest price for your life, by giving the life of His dear Son Jesus Christ for you. You did not earn salvation; it is purely His love that provides it for you. How can He stop loving you when you are now His child? As much as you did not work for His love to be saved, even now you do not earn His love by your works. He just loves you, trust Him.

Trust when battling heaviness

Tic tac tic tac
The watch is ticking, time is going forward
My life is standing still
At times I take many steps backwards
My heart sinks in floods
My head drowns in sorrow
But time is not standing
Seconds are leading to minutes
To hours, days, weeks, months

Heaviness is my enemy
That comes uninvited
I have to clear my mind
Otherwise, its oppressors will keep it bound
Only hope is my hope
Yes, I have to keep looking,
I have to keep seeing ahead
I may not know where I am going
But I trust the hand that holds me
It is the eternal hand that created the universe
I can take refuge in its guidance

I refuse to stay in the darkness
Instead, I choose to see the light from afar
For my guider has promised
That I will see His goodness in the land of the living
Knowing that He never lies is my comfort
That I put on as a blanket

I trust the hand that holds me
Though I may not see the way
I will keep on moving forward
For this hand will never let me go.

Real Life Testimony

'When I lost my trust in God I honestly thought that He did not care, He did not love me enough to care about what I was going through. When I saw His love, when I began to acknowledge His love for me, I began to trust that in spite of my circumstances He is working out a way out for me behind the scenes'.

- FOUR -

Flourishing like a Palm Tree

The palm tree is said to be flourishing, because it grows higher yet deeper than many trees, with evergreen leaves despite harsh unfavourable weather conditions. In the dessert you will find it well-nourished, be it winter or summer the leaves will not lose colour. When strong winds come, it bends to the direction of the wind, after the wind, it returns to its posture and keeps blowing its leaves.

The secret of the palm is in the roots. When other trees quickly mushroom from little moisture and show up to grow above, the palm goes deeper with its roots. It is not satisfied with shallow waters; the roots seek for streams of water that run from the rocks underneath the earth. It will keep extending its roots until they reach that pure, cold, refreshing water from the rock. When trees planted with it have long shown up, it comes up last. But it will only show up when it is satisfied that the roots are well-nourished. Hence whether in winter or summer, in solitude or dessert, the palm will flourish. The secret is in the roots.

When you face tough conditions as a Christian, they are not there to destroy you.

They are there to lead you to cast your roots deeper. The usual prayers, fellowship and all other spiritual activities that were keeping you watered are no longer enough to keep you satiated. When you feel your strength-sapping away even when you have not done anything wrong or different, that is time to cast your roots deeper. That is time to move from living by excitement and motivations to having a deeper substantiated relationship with the father.

The kind of relationship in casting your roots deeper is not dependent on wind, hail or storm. It is not based on noise, dance or miracles. It is a conversation with a deep small voice that calls you to seclusion. The voice that takes you from the excitement and noise to a quiet place. It pushes you to push beyond drama to the point of knowing, intimately, that God is your God. The dessert, the heat, the frustration, they are all pushing you to this point.

In order to survive, you have to have a hiding place.

You have to know how God speaks to you. You have to identify the lead of God and the hand of God. You learn to dwell in His presence without goosebumps or dramatic shakings, but by knowing that you know that He is there, He hears you, and He attends to your call.

In this level, your faith transcends, your prayer life deepens, you move from senses to spiritual. This is the building of a palm tree. Beyond this point, you are able to flourish, despite circumstances you flourish in the courts of God. It is dangerous to live your whole life without getting to this level, as you will be a seasonal believer all your life. The cost of flourishing is in deepening of your roots. The push to deepen your roots is tribulation.

'Consider it pure joy, my brothers and sisters, whenever you face trials of many kinds, because you know that the testing of your faith produces perseverance.'
James 1:2-3 (NIV).

It seemed you would not make it; it seemed you had reached your end. In reality, you were transformed into a deeper dimension of your faith where you will no longer be moved by winds or storms. This is the dimension where you are able to confidently say;

> *'For I am convinced that neither death nor life ... will be able to separate us from the love of God that is in Christ Jesus our Lord.'*
> *Romans 8:38-39 (NIV).*

> *Oh Lord God, I thank you*
> *For when the floods*
> *Swallowed me up, your Love*
> *like a strong wave lifted me higher*
> *and led me to the shore*
> *Where I said I have found my rest*
> *For in your presence is my rest.*

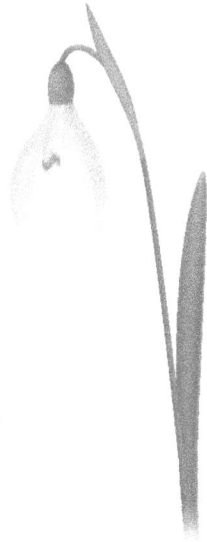

- FIVE -

Through The Wilderness

There is no call with the multitudes. You cannot hear the voice of God while you are in commotion. When everyone departs, that is time to draw near God. That is time to learn to hear His voice, to strengthen the relationship and to find His guidance. This is when you are trained to be in warfare and prevail. You cannot run to call someone to fight on your behalf because you are on your own. It is your chance for God to train your hands to war. This is when God's children stop running for help whenever trouble comes. They learn that they have to use the authority given to them when they received Christ in their lives.

David was alone when the lion and the bear came to attack the sheep. There was no one to run to, so he had to call on God and face the lion and the bear. When he was facing Goliath, he was already trained and ready for the task. Goliath was just a set stage for him to ascend to greatness, but the training had taken place in the wilderness.

'But David said to Saul, "Your servant was tending his father's sheep. When a lion or a bear came and took a lamb from the flock, I went out after him and attacked him, and rescued it from his mouth; and when he rose up against me, I seized him by his beard and struck him and killed him. Your servant has killed both the lion and the bear; and this uncircumcised Philistine will be like one of them, since he has taunted the armies of the living God.' 1 Samuel 17:34-36 (NASB).

Moses sensed that there was greatness in him, he tried to express it, but it got him into trouble to a point where he had to run for his life.

He then had to spend most of his life in the wilderness, tending the sheep. God did not visit Moses in the palace, or even in Jethro's house.

Moses had an encounter with God in the wilderness; it was when he was alone that God revealed Himself to him and commissioned him.

'Now Moses was tending the flock of Jethro his father-in-law, the priest of Midian, and he led the flock to the far side of the wilderness and came to Horeb, the mountain of God. There the angel of the Lord appeared to him in flames of fire from within a bush....' Exodus 3:1-2 (NIV).

Your wilderness prepares you for your greatness

If you have been crying that you are alone and have no one to turn to, it is not a mistake; it is a setup. The world may seem to have forgotten you, but God wants to prepare you for the next chapter of your life.

Everyone in Egypt probably forgot about Moses; some may have even believed that he was dead. When he came back to Egypt, he was a different Moses. He was no longer a boy from the palace, but a man called and highly anointed by God. the transformation to one of the greatest prophets that ever lived took place in the wilderness. In the wilderness of loneliness, it is where you learn to draw from the well within you: 'Whoever believes in Me, as the Scripture has said:

'Streams of living water will flow from within him'
- John 7:38 (BSB).

There is an inner strength that you only realise when you have no one else to call but God. You have God-given resources and abilities that you do not know about until you find yourself in the wilderness and you are alone. When no one is your voice of reason, you get channelled to hear the voice of God, as He is the only one you can talk to. There is a purpose for the season of loneliness in your life, go beyond the pain of being alone to discover God's ultimate plan for your life.

I have cried for loneliness and for sorrow
I have shed tears of regret and cried for being rejected
I have cried because of struggle, loss, plus
Disappointments, pain and sufferings
But I've never had to cry for being left by You
Through thick and thin You have been with me
You have carried me, wiped tears from my eyes
And given me a smile
You have given me reason to rise and face each day
My pillar, my hope, my God
Indeed, You are a friend that sticks closer than a brother.

When Weary, Find Rest

Tiredness and fatigue are a reality in life. No matter how well-meaning, disciplined and determined we are, life is a long journey. Have you realised that life is not fair? You have been sweet to everyone but have been treated harshly. You have been honest and pure in your heart, but got misunderstood and backstabbed. You have been there for everyone to the best of your ability, but have found yourself alone, with no one to even shed the burden of your heart with.

All of a sudden, you feel weary. What used to be a joy becomes a burden. Your energy slips away; you are too tired. You want to pray, but you ask yourself for how long? How long should you keep that prayer item on, how long should you hope things will get better? You reach a point of having to drag yourself to take care of your children. You lose the desire to go to your job. You keep thinking 'I am just tired'. How many times do you have such a thought, but tell yourself you need to be strong, you need to pull on, for the sake of your family, for the sake of your children, for the sake of your employer, for the sake...for the sake. Yes, it is for the sake of everyone and everything else but yourself.

Brethren, it is okay to take a seat down and rest when you are weary. Yes, it is okay to have a week, a month or however long it takes to do nothing except being with yourself. It is okay to take an adult gap year to replenish your soul.

It is okay to take a break, be responsible for nothing and no one, except the breath you take.

Tiredness is not a weakness; it is an indication of a long journey that has been walked, of battles that have been fought and of energy well spent. You are weary because you have been walking uphill. You are weary because you have been carrying a heavy load for long. You are weary because you have been fighting internal and external battles. The natural thing to do after a fight, a long walk or run is to rest. Why then do we feel like failures when we take a break in the midst of our life journey? It is prerogative that we do the same as in any other situation, sit down and rest. Your family will be fine; your children will do well; actually, nothing will stop functioning. The good news is, the rest you take revitalises, sharpens, refreshes, re-energizes and delivers a stronger version of yourself.

In a nutshell, the very same people and reasons you push for, are the main beneficiaries of a revitalized and revived you.

Have enough courage to rest from your daily duties, whether in secular, private or ministry. Have the courage to take a break, think nothing and just look at the beauty of nature. Listen to sounds of music, seek for laughter and have no other responsibility. Go to prayer to do nothing else but worship God, and forget about everything else you have been requesting for years and have not been answered. Worship Him for who He is, after that go and play. This is the best mental and spiritual care you can give yourself.

'But they that wait upon the Lord shall renew their strength; they shall mount up with wings as eagles; they shall run, and not be weary; and they shall walk, and not faint.'
Isaiah 40:31 (KJV).

Weariness, pain and life sorrows entangle our spirits so much, before we know it we are under a shadow that is difficult to break free from. Once we are enveloped with darkness, it is very difficult to see the light again. Therefore, we should be ahead, never allowing a point of being consumed by the cares and worries of this world. In this highly busy generation, where even quietness is not really quietness as we then switch to social media, we need to be deliberate about rest. We need to be deliberate about letting go and allowing ourselves to be refreshed. That is the only way of keeping ourselves mentally healthy and revived to carry on with our life purpose.

What to do when you feel depleted, and all hope is gone?

When you cannot see the light, all you see ahead is darkness, what you do is important as it determines how you make it to the other end of your struggles.

1. Surround yourself with positive people.

It is easy to be surrounded by people who feel like you, as you will have a similar language. The danger is no one will lift another up. This is time to rather be around those who are feeling positive about life, who will speak life to you. Those who are currently having dreams and sharing their vision about tomorrow. Those who are currently sharing testimonies of how God has pulled them out, and how they are seeing breakthroughs. All this will lift your spirit and will bear testimony to you that your own testimony is next.

2. Take time out

This has been discussed in length above. You cannot keep pushing yourself when there is nothing left within you. You need to replenish and regain strength to carry on with your life.

3. Take each day as it comes

When you are facing harsh situations, it is difficult to think ahead. Whenever you look ahead, you see darkness and gloom. When your dreams are shattered looking ahead just breaks you down, because you no longer see where you are going, to the point of seeing no reason to be alive. So try not to think long term. Avoid trying to look at one year or more for now. Avoid thinking of how you will be in five years, instead think short term. Wake up each morning and thank God that you are alive. Think of what you will be doing today even if it's just taking a walk and doing minimal tasks.

4. Separate each issue you are facing as a standalone problem

When you look at all your issues as one, you will be overwhelmed. Even thinking of solutions will tire you out. But, when you break down all the challenges, write them down to their own separate entities, you are then able to have them as separate issues in your mind. Attending to each issue at a time will be easier and more manageable during this time.

5. Find something to do

In difficult times when our morale is down, we do not want to do anything. You rather be in bed the whole day. You hardly have energy, and even things you used to like doing don't matter anymore. There is one thing that you can commit to doing – help someone. Think of acts of kindness that you can do each day. You may not feel like doing much, but small things you can involve yourself in, especially to assist those who are less privileged, will go a long way. At the beginning such involvements will feel like pain, but in a matter of days you will be looking forward to this, and at the end of the day you will have something to you look forward to, and you will feel good about it and yourself. Nothing feels more rewarding than bringing a smile in someone's face; this will go a long way in lifting you up during times of discouragement.

Beyond Physical Senses

It takes more than human strength to push through the thick dark clouds of sadness and see the rainbow. When the heart is enveloped with sadness, and the mind can only see hollow darkness; it takes the hand of God to lift your head beyond that shroud and keep going. These are times where you just have to walk, whether you see the way or not, whether you have direction or not. Even when there is no hope for the next hour or the next day, you just keep going. In times of being surrounded by darkest clouds, there is a sucking of will and determination that leaves you with no desire to start a new day. Giving in to that cloud is the beginning of a most unbearable tumbling into a pit of darkness that literally has no end, but one keeps sinking and has no strength to pull out of it.

When an aircraft takes off on a gloomy rainy day, all you see above you are dark clouds. But, the pilot keeps moving the craft higher, even when it gets bumpy. Once the pilot manages to pull through the clouds, you find yourself in a different world. In a matter of a few minutes you have moved from that bumpy dark space to sunshine, now you look at those clouds below you.

That is what the divine hand of God does. When you have reached the end of human strength, will power, a reason to live; that hand can pull you through the dark clouds.

You can still rise up and smile, wake up and do your daily business. The circumstances have not changed, but a divine pilot has taken over. You don't have direction, but you just keep going. Suddenly you find yourself seeing some little bit of hope and possibility. That is what happens when we surrender to God in the most challenging moments.

The truth is, what human strength cannot do, when human strength fails you, you need to surrender to divinity. At the point of breaking, call on God. You do not have to feel Him for Him to be there; He is Spirit. In toughest of times you don't feel Him with physical senses but when you have called, just know that He is there. Your senses will not see immediate evidence. Tough times are not for senses when darkness wants you to give in; it is time to shift from senses to the Spirit. In time, when you have called on God, you will pull through to the other side of darkness.

It may not mean the clouds are gone, but it means you are able to soar above them, you just cruise with the supernatural strength. After a long while, you will look back and wonder how on earth you made it. You then realise that it was God. You did not feel Him, but now you can see that He was there.

You are not without help. Call on God. Call on Him in times of trouble.

The power of the seed is in its burial
In darkness, weight and moist
That is where the seed swells to the point
Of bursting. Then boom,
New life has begun; it has been multiplied!
Moments of darkness, silence and gloom
Are the worst moments in life;
But that is where the real you is birthed
Just when you think it's over, at the point of dying to self,
You emerge.

Best Days Ahead

Do not conclude about me yet, I have not reached my end.

My destiny is known by my creator.

Don't be mistaken to think you've seen the end product, I'm still work in progress.

To you who have been written off, who've been given names, who've been buried alive and nothing is expected from you, today take heart. What may have seemed like the end is actually the beginning of a new chapter.

Do not allow conclusions reached about you to bury you.

As long as the Lord lives, you still have hope, your dreams can be a reality, you shall see the goodness of the Lord in the land of the living.

Man's conclusion is not God's conclusion about you. Keep on believing, your best days are still ahead.

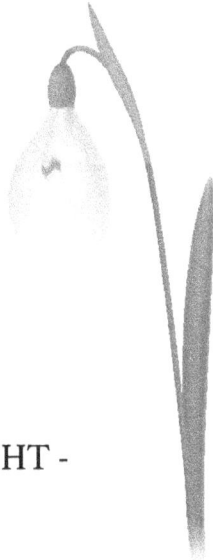

- EIGHT -

Stars in the Night

The stars are always there in the sky; they do not come and go. The reason we do not see them during the day is that daylight is way brighter; therefore, it dims the stars. It is in the night that we see and appreciate light from the stars. It may look pitch dark when you are in the house, but when you go out, you appreciate the distant light of the stars, they make beauty to behold and appreciate.

During the night season of our lives, there are stars we should learn to appreciate. If you can sit down in the midst of your hardships and consciously recall what God has done for you, you will realise you have blessings to count, even in hardships. These are types of blessing we take for granted when things are fine because the sun is shining, there is so much more good happening in our lives. But in the darkness, you are able to appreciate that you had something to eat. Others around you take that for granted, but if you have no source of income that mere provision is a blessing to you. We appreciate that no one in the family got ill, as we did not have the means to take them to medical facilities.

You appreciate some unexpected help, random favours. Those are the stars in your night.

One of the best ways to lift your spirit and remind yourself of God's goodness in hard times is to count your blessings. They may not stand out or come easily to your memory, but if you take time to look, there are blessings. Remember that blind people wish they had sight to be able to read like you.

Someone out there wishes they were able to walk, they don't even mind not running, if only they could walk. Someone wishes they had just one child. There is so much to be grateful for. When you do your gratitude check, you will realise that the more you lift gratitude to God, the more you raise your hope for things He is still going to do for you, even if it's just giving you one more day.

What is one thing that God has done for you today? How about this week? Take a moment out of your thoughts and write down in a piece of paper, just one thing you are grateful for. Do not stop until you remember, including the gift of life. After writing it down, present it before God as you would present a prayer request. I know you have important issues to pray about, you may be in need of a speedy miracle. But as you read this, just take that moment, lift your written gratitude to God and from the bottom of your heart, say 'father I thank you, there is no God like you. Only you could have done this for me. I am grateful.'

**I believe there is more than one of those tiny stars
that are shinning in your night.**

Do not ignore them, behold and appreciate them. they are
part of the reminder that it's only a night, your day is coming.
They are also a reminder that good things have been
happening for you, even when you were not paying
attention to them, there has always been miracles here and
there to show you that God is still there.

- NINE -

Keep Sowing

We have spoken about how much we feel overwhelmed during the hard times of our lives. But it is very important that you never completely stop sowing, meaning do not stop doing something towards your dreams. Remember, no matter how sad we are, life does not stop, time keeps going. It is true that we go through painful circumstances, and all we want to do sometimes is just to lie down and think of our sorrows. Sadly, if we were to be sad and do nothing during that period, we have lost that period of our lives for good. Time is one resource that once lost, can never be recovered.

On the other hand, if we push through our feelings and keep sowing, keep working on whatever that is workable, we are able to turn what was meant for evil to work for our good. That is where we realise the strength that we spoke about in earlier chapters, the strength born out of hardships.

> *'Those who sow in tears Shall reap in joy. He who continuously goes forth weeping, Bearing seed for sowing, Shall doubtless come again with rejoicing, bringing his sheaves with him'*

Psalm 126:5-6 (NKJV).

This biblical principle uses a narrative of a farmer. A farmer who keeps going to the field to sow even in unfavourable circumstances will doubtless have a harvest. The principle of sowing and reaping cannot be broken. No matter how much the pain it takes for this farmer, but if he keeps doing what he needs to do to put a seed on the ground, he will celebrate with a harvest, even if the conditions of planting were harsh.

In hardship, try your level best not to fold hands. Many times we pray and hope for the answer. But God needs something in our hands to work out the miracle we need.

The question has always been, 'what do you have in your hand'?

God uses what is there to produce what is not there. Many Christians live disappointed lives because they prayed, cried and took a back seat and waited for a miracle; they never realised that they were part of the miracle.

I studied and completed my senior degree in the most painful moments of my life. No one saw that I was going through hardship when I was in class. I looked like everybody else. But at night I was crying. While crying, I would do my assignments and study. I had ongoing insomnia, and every night would be up by 1 am. While in tears, I decided to write and finish my first book during that time. On the year of graduation, I had finished both my Master's degree and published my first book.

If I had slept throughout that season and re- fused to do anything and just listened to my pain, no one would have blamed me; it would have been understandable.

As much as this was the most painful period for me, it became the most productive season of my life. Do not allow tears to put your life on a standstill, while in that pain, what can your hand do? Find it and do it; your victory in the midst of pain will trigger a turnaround moment for your life. Think about it, what can you do right now to turn your season of tears into a celebration?

'Passing through the valley of Weeping they make is a place of springs; Yea; the early rain covereth it with blessings'
Psalm 84:6 (ASV).

These are good news; you do not have to wait for the morning before you celebrate. This is where the heroes are born, when you pass through the place of tears and make it a place of celebration. When you were supposed to break down and become history, you can make that very place your history maker, your turning point. You cannot change the circumstances you are facing, but you can do something that will change the course of your life right there in the midst of trouble.

> **'If you wait until the wind and the weather are just right, you will never plant anything and never harvest anything.'**
> *Ecclesiastes 11:4 (GNT).*

Don't wait for a brighter day; do what you can do now to bring a brighter day for you and your family.

Real Life Testimony

I learned what is in this chapter from my parents. My mother took herself to school through short term jobs from the age of 13 until a teacher's certificate. She either worked in fields for money, or worked as a maid. She had a dream to be a teacher. Poverty and restrictions for girl children to get an education did not stop her. Nothing fa- voured her schooling, but she did it anyways, through lack, ridicule, she achieved her dream career.

Fast forward, if my mother had waited for good days none of us her children would have had tertiary qualifications. It was against all odds, in difficult unfavourable circumstances that she sent us to tertiary institutions. There was no money, with female teacher's salaries being peanuts at the time. With all of us, she would knock on various doors, from first year till we completed. She had a dream of all her children being professionals. Circumstances were not permitting. She sowed in tears, then her dream was realised.

My father was a farmer. I do not remember my father sitting and not working in the field, except for rainy days. Summer or winter he had something to do. In winter seasons he would fetch water from the nearest dam and water all the plants continuously. As a result, my father's fields always yielded a harvest, in season and out of season. This was a wonder to many people. What they did not realise was that in an unfavourable season, he kept working. So he had one harvest or the other all year round, and his fields were always green in winter or summer. He placed a demand on the ability of the ground to yield to the seed, and did not allow cold and harsh conditions to determine his harvest.

- TEN -

When the Morning Comes

You are bigger than your current circumstances.

Life is more than what you see now.

See a bigger picture.

There is much more beyond your today.

If today is your worst day ever,

it does not mean your life has ended.

Present needs and struggles may bring all focus to the now,
magnifying the struggles and blocking any light ahead.

But rest assured, there's still a better tomorrow, a future and a hope.

In the eye of your mind look, see a brighter future.

'...weeping may endure for a night, but joy com- eth in the morning'
Psalm 30:5 (NKJV).

No matter how long the night lasts, morning will come. It is illegal for a night to continue into the day. God created day and night, no matter how long the night enjoys its own presence, when it is time for the day it has to give way. Actually, darkness does not really just leave on its own, but light breaks forth, and darkness has to disappear for the light is more powerful than darkness.

When it is time for light to shine in your life, nothing can stop it.

When your day breaks no darkness can stop it. There will never be a time where the day is skipped so that the night continues in the time allocated for the day. You may feel like the night season in your life has lasted forever, but rest assured that the dawn is about to break, your morning is near. This is the law set by God, and nothing can change it.

How do you know the morning has come in your life? It starts in the inside of you. You experience the dawning of a new day within you first before circumstances on the outside change. When you feel a bulb of hope switching in your heart, when you begin to 'see' with the eye of your mind. All along you saw darkness, and you were hopeless, all of a sudden you see some light, you have some dream playing in your imagination, and your mind is seeing better things than what you are facing. All of a sudden, you feel hope rise in you, and you begin to have life and expectation within you. Nothing has changed on the external, but there is a shift in your internal environment, that is an indication.

God said to Jeremiah:

> *'Jeremiah, what do you see? And I said, "I see a branch of an almond tree." Then the Lord said to me 'you have seen well, for I am ready to perform my word.'*
> *Jeremiah 1:11-12 (NKJV).*

We do not know what Jeremiah was seeing all along, but now he saw well, he saw an indication that something new is happening, there was a new thing springing forth.

It is important to discern the seasons. When dawn comes, it is time to wake up and go to the field. The night kept you confined; you were restrained and kept in one position. When dawn breaks, you have to come out, take your 'tools' and begin to work.

One may say, 'I have been trying all this with no success, why should I try again?' You should try again because now is the day. You have been putting effort, but the season was not in your favour. When you put that effort again in the right season, you will be surprised at the results. Pray the prayers you have been praying again, don't say it has been years God would have answered by now, no, pray again. The day time is the time where doors open with less effort; where long-stand- ing issues give way to your breakthrough in a moment. This is the perfect time to re-engage your spiritual warfare because this is the season of answers.

The day is breaking in your life. The season has shifted. No sorrow can last forever.

If you have been having such hard times that you wondered where God is, He is still on the throne, and His word still remains. That season of difficulty, no matter how long it stayed, has to give in to the next season of your life. Don't die in the night, just hold on a little bit longer, your day is about to break.

The Lord's Time

As no man can stop the eruption of a volcano,
So no one can stop God's plan for your life
In the natural, all may seem quiet
But in the Spirit, there is a move,
There is alignment; there is accumulation,
There is brewing; the heat is multiplying,
Something is about to explode to your favour
You are breaking forth; you will be unstoppable,
It is the Lord's doing, and none can stop it in its time!

- ELEVEN -

Never Forsaken

He clothes my shame with honour

Covers my nakedness with goodness

So that in my weakness He is my strength, my shelter in the rain The ever-present, everlasting, magnificent Father, Friend, Lord He seats Lord above all, yet He

Holds my hand as an ever-present help When all turn away and forget,

He never forgets me

He remembers my prayers, He remembers

My silent pleas, and He remembers His promises to me
Time may change, people may go,

Circumstances may change But I am not forsaken, My God

Is with me always, His love is eternal I am never forsaken

'Can a woman forget her nursing child, And not have compassion on the son of her womb? Sure- ly they may forget, Yet I will not forget you.'
Isaiah 49:15 (NKJV)

When you feel you are alone, you feel you are forgotten, and there is no more space in life for you; there is one person who has not forgotten you. He remembers your prayers, your giving, your dedication, your love. Even if you have lost it all, He remembers. It is a matter of time; the season will change for your favour. It may have taken years or months of sorrows, but yet still He has not forgotten you.

You say you have done all you could do; you have fought the fight of faith the best way you know. Before you throw in the towel, do one last thing, STAND. You are not forgotten; you are not alone. Yes, you used to feel Him, and you don't anymore, remember God transcends the physical senses. You have the best assurance ever that cannot be shaken, His word. You are not forsaken, trust God and keep standing. Your breakthrough is on the horizon.

An expected end.

God gave each person an expected end. He designed it in the DNA, in thought patterns, in mental intrinsic imaginations each person has it and it differs from the rest. Expectations can be disappointed. Circumstances, the unexpected, life complications can disappoint the one with an expectation.

But if we lay the expected end at the feet of the One who gave it, He surely can preserve it, protect it and ensure that all the unexpected mishaps turn around to work for the good. So that eventually whatever was meant to divert, destroy, distract, abort, deny; whether it be fire, storms, rejection, persecution...it will still work for the realisation of the expected end.

Now that is the unfathomable wisdom of God!

'For I know the thoughts that I think toward you, saith the Lord, thoughts of peace, and not of evil, to give you an expected end.'
Jeremiah 29:11 (KJV).

Song of Jubilee

When you see my laughter don't wish to be like me
Because you don't know how many tears I have shed

When you see my success, don't wish we could switch
places But wonder if you could have survived my failures

When you see me walking on my mountain tops Don't
think 'life is easy for her'

Because you will never fathom the depth Of my valley,
even if I could relate it to you

When you see a constant bright spark, light step, Smile on
my face, sunshine all around me,

Instead of wishing you were in my shoes right now, Think
if you could have enjoyed being in my shoes When my face
wore sadness, when I was surrounded With darkness, when
heaviness swallowed me up

Instead of wishing to be me, be happy for me

That God brought me through. Be content with what you are, because what I am came with a price the smile I have is a product of many tears the crown I wear is a product of my thorns the success I have is a product of many disappointments the mountain top I am standing on is a product of much pain, heartache and failure!

- TWELVE -

The Process of Becoming

There is always a gap between where you are and the future you see. In order to get to that future, there are steps to be taken, and if any of those steps are jumped, it jeopardises the perfection of the picture that you see. Some of the steps seem like a nuisance, some seem unreasonable, some seem like they do more harm than good. That is the process of becoming. You have the call, you have the vision, you have the great dream of who you were made to be, but you will walk towards becoming that person.

Most of us get excited once we catch a glimpse of the greatness God has in store for us. We hardly entertain any thought that it may be in the future. Whether we receive this glimpse through prophecy, in our own imagination or through being prayed for, we are likely to expect it to happen as quickly as possible. We wait in expectation and antic-

ipation. However, most of the time we wait until we wonder as often there is a stretch where our lives rather take an opposite direction than what we were expecting. As believers, we get disappointed, as all excitement and expectation gets replaced by anxiety and questioning whether we did indeed hear from the Lord to the point of letting go of that life we had anticipated.

If you find yourself in this position, just remember one thing, God declares the end from the beginning. Isaiah 46:10 (ESV) says "declaring the end from the beginning and from ancient times things not yet done, saying, 'My counsel shall stand, and I will accomplish all my purpose'". He who cannot lie created you with a powerful destiny, and He has the power and the ability to make it a reality. In fact, everything you need to achieve that destiny is already within you; the process you are going through is schooling you to tap into that which is already within you. At times it is the preparation of your character, and at times is strengthening you to have the capacity to carry the greatness you are about to step into.

To understand the greatness, you carry, you have to understand the greatness of God, in whose image you are created. You also have to understand the power that came to reside on you when you received the Lord Jesus Christ, which is the same power that raised Christ from the dead! You carry that power; you walk in that power. Moreover, you have a backup of the heavenly hosts; you need to understand the ministry of the Holy Spirit, the ministry of the angelic hosts and all divine order at your disposal. All you need is the revelation of all this providence, once your eyes of understanding are open to this, you will realise that you are unstoppable. You are a time bomb waiting to happen; you are a miracle in waiting for the right moment. You are in the likeness of God, and even if you only possess a fraction of His capability, it is enough to bring this whole universe to recognise that you are indeed a son of God. He would never give any part of Himself to manifest inferior to who He is because every gift and ability we possess is to and for His glory.

Therefore, rest assured that your future is still as God has promised you. All the opposition you have been experiencing is just your own process of becoming that person. When you get to your destination, nothing and no one can take it away from you.

One day you will ask God, "Why did you not tell me that this is the beautiful end you had for me? I would have endured my hardships better; I would have complained less and believed more."

And God will say, "That is why I gave you faith, so that you could not live on what you saw but on what you did not see. I needed you to trust that your end would be better than your beginning, I needed you to see with the eye of my word that I have given you."

Then you will say, "Oh wow, now I see. But why did I have to go through all that mess for that long?"

God will say, "Take a look at the butterfly, all animals admire it. Unfortunately, they cannot just wake up and portray that beauty. You know why? Because it took a butterfly to be a larva (caterpillar), then a pupa, then finally became a fully-fledged butterfly becoming a beauty and a wonder. It didn't just happen overnight, so it is the same with you. You were not formed overnight, but every step you went through made you who you are today, and nobody else can be like you."

Each and every battle you have faced was training and preparing you for where you are going. No experience is too small; they all count towards your assignment. After all has been said and done, when the puzzle of your destiny begins to make sense, you will look back with a smile and say 'it was worth it'.

Look at the life of Joseph. He dreamt of his greatness while he was a child. Yet there was a process that seemed very contrary to what he had seen about his life. But until today, everyone is learning about the greatness he became.

What about the life of David, who got anointed at his youth? But there was a process of becoming that great King. He went through it all, to a point where he is referred to a man after God's own heart.

Who can you think of today, in our present-day and age? Many great people in our recent history have been through that journey of becoming. God can't wait to also celebrate with you when you get to your destination! Wherever you may be in your path, each step is getting you closer.

Purpose Calls

In the midst of chaos, it calls.

In the midst of tribulation and struggle, the voice of purpose is heard. Purpose does not wait for a perfect day. It does not wait for calm. While you fight, while you sweat, while you face storms, when your dream needs to be birthed, you should push it forth.

Canaan was not announced when slavery stopped, in the midst of grue- some slavery, they were called out to Canaan.

Do not silence the voice of your destiny.

No matter what you are in the midst of when that voice calls respond, when it's time to deliver get up and give birth.

The elevation of David did not come in peace, the kingly anointing of David did not manifest in peaceful times, it was during a serious war that it manifested.

The Process of Becoming

Your next level will be ushered while life is happening.

May you find the strength to break forth, grasp your purpose and be ush- ered into your promised land.

THIRTEEN

Winner's Attitude

Take me where the Eagles dwell

Let me soar with wings to the heights of the earth

Let me not dwell where there is bickering and murmuring
Let me not dwell where there is limitation of the eye

My vision is meant to pierce through the storms and see
mountain tops

Valleys are not meant to be my home

Show me the Eagle's nests in the heights of the wind, for it
is where I belong

The storms are meant to carry me higher to where I belong
I am meant to wrap myself in the thunder and lightning
And allow them to transform me to the elegance of
dominion and excellence

I do not run for cover in harsh condition

It is in those conditions where the magnificent power of my
strength excels

With sheer determination built within me,

I stretch my wings and soar to where I belong For I belong
with the Eagles

You may be in your lowest right now, but that is not where you belong. Hope works hand in hand with faith (Hebrews 11:1). Hope is a desire and expectation of something good in the future. Hope lifts your eyes from your present circumstances to what will be. Faith brings that expectation to the now and ensures that what we hope for becomes a reality. The natural mind may ask how these things you hope for will come to pass, considering your current circumstances. But God's word says,

"You won't feel any wind or see any rain, but there will be plenty of water for you and your animals"
2 Kings 3:17 (CEV)

God is not limited to our natural resources, when you add faith to hope the supernatural takes over and produce that which is naturally impossible.

All winners have two things in common, they have hope, and they focus on the end product. They do not deny the process, but they have an undeterred focus to the end goal, and it propels them to keep going.

Before an athlete starts running, he looks at the finish line. In his mind, he sees himself striking the finish line; he already sees the cheer and celebration as he reaches that line. He pre-lives the celebration and that excitement of victory. As he runs, at times having to jump the hurdles, he does not even register those jumps he needs to make, in his mind, he just sees the end.

Hurdles in life are a given, as outlined throughout the book. Now the question is, are you going to adopt the winner's attitude? Are you going to be the winner that you are already meant to be? Whatever obstacles you come across they have not been given authority to undo your end, your name is already on the finish line.

Every person has two crowds that are cheering them. One crowd is cheering you to go back and to give up. It reminds you of your past difficulties; it reminds you of your family history. It tells you that no one made it before you, why do you think it will be different with you. It reminds you of your weaknesses, how you do not have what it takes. It tells you to stop making a fool of yourself, to accept what life has turned out to be and to adjust to your circumstances. That crowd even shows you of other people you know, and how they accepted their fate and stopped chasing what was seemingly impossible to them, it tells you that accept your reality. Unfortunately, this crowd has the loudest of voices, as these scream in your mind, in your circumstances and even through certain people that you know.

But there is another crowd that is cheering you. That is the crowd the bible refers to as the 'cloud of witnesses'. This crowd tells you that it is possible. It says your beginning does not determine your end, for the end of a thing is better than its beginning (Ecclesiastes 7:8). It tells you that so many people made it, against all the odds, they reached their destination. It reminds you of the heroes of faith, both in the present and in the past. It reminds you of your previous victories, and that if God did it before He will do it again. It reminds you of your strengths, the talents you carry and the gifts you have that they are meant to be lived in full, while in this side of eternity. It reminds you that no matter what the enemy can try, he can never change the plan of God for your life.

"As for us, we have this large crowd of witnesses around us. So then, let us rid ourselves of every- thing that gets in the way, and of the sin which holds on to us so tightly, and let us run with determination the race that lies before us"

Hebrews 12:1 (GNT)

That is the crowd that is cheering us. Some are saints that lived before us; who passed through fires, slavery, all kinds of persecution, but finished their race. Some are living with us in this age; they have seen it all, been through hunger, ridicule and all kinds of suffering, some ran for their lives in times of wars, and they never saw their families again, but they have reached their mountain top. With God, these saints did get to their destined lives despite all hardships, so will you.

Winner's traits

I. Winners take counsel.

Winners are not afraid to seek for counsel, because

> ***"Without counsel, plans fail, but with many advisers they succeed"***
> *Proverbs 15:22 (ESV)*

When you are in misery, and you do not know what to do, someone has been in your position before. Their advice will be valuable. Certain frustrations and losses can be avoided with proper advice.

2. Winners never stop learning.

Even at the level of an expert, there is still something new to be learnt. Where growth stops, decay begins. As long as we are alive, we need to be growing in one area or another, learning will lead to growth.

3. Winners are not afraid to start all over again.

No matter how many times you have fallen, the winning attitude leads you to stand up and try one more time. All the failures are never wasted, they become experience. The only way of knowing what works and what does not work is that unwanted failure.

4. Winners never quit.

So it has been said over and over, and this still remains as a cornerstone of success. If one door closes, winners look for another door. If an attempt fails, winners go back to the drawing board, restrategise and go for it again. The attitude of winning says: keep asking, keep knocking, keep seeking (Luke 11:9-13). A no today does not mean a no tomorrow, never quit!

There is no question about your destiny; it was set before you were born. Choose the right crowd to cheer you and pay attention to what it says. Choose the right voice to be the loudest in your mind and spirit, let if fuel you to put aside all the hurdles and aim for the destination. Allow your mind to see the finish line, and let that picture in your mind be ignited by your faith in the living God. That is the attitude of winners. No matter what today is, as you keep pressing forward, it is a given that your tomorrow will be what God designed it to be.

Your Word For This Season

For you will be like a rose that Springs up in the desert. Your beauty

Shines bright as a rainbow. People will wonder at how you glimmer with glory

So bright it blinds the eye You grew up in the wilderness

You will have life where there is no water Where there is death all around you, you shine forth Where there is no moist supply you flourish with life

For God is your source

Jehovah is the holder and the supplier of your life

Your chains are breaking on their own accord, they will be broken forever

You break-out from your imprisonment You dance and sing in celebration

For your light break forth in the night as a morning star Your day and season of breakthrough is here

- FOURTEEN -

God's Promises to Refresh Your Soul

Though the fig tree does not bud and there are no grapes on the vines, though the olive crop fails, and the fields produce no food, though there are no sheep in the pen and no cattle in the stalls, yet I will rejoice in the Lord, I will be joyful in God my Saviour.

Habakkuk 3:17-18 (NIV).

When you go through deep waters, I will be with you. When you go through rivers of dif- ficulty, you will not drown. When you walk through the fire of oppression, you will not be burned up; the flames will not consume you.

Isaiah 43:2 (NLT).

I would have lost heart, unless I had believed That I would see the goodness of the LORD in the land of the living.

Psalm 27:13 (NKJV)

And we know that in all things God works for the good of those who love Him, who have been called according to His purpose.
Romans 8:28 (NIV).

Many are the afflictions of the righteous, but the LORD delivers him out of them all.
Psalm 34:19 (NKJV).

Be strong and of good courage, do not fear nor be afraid of them; for the LORD your God, He is the One who goes with you. He will not leave you nor forsake you.

Deuteronomy 31:6 (NKJV).

May the Lord answer you in the day of trouble; May the name of the God of Jacob defend you; May He send you help from the sanctuary, and strengthen you out of Zion.

Psalm 20:1-2

Tell the righteous it will be well with them, for they will enjoy the fruit of their deeds.

Isaiah 3:10 (NIV).

For no one is cast off by the Lord forever.Though he brings grief, he will show compas- sion, so great is his unfailing love. For he does not willingly bring affliction or grief to anyone.

Lamentations 3:31-33 (NIV).

Yea, though I walk through the valley of the shadow of death, I will fear no evil; for You are with me; Your rod and Your staff, they comfort me. ... Surely goodness and mercy shall follow me All the days of my life; And I will dwell in the house of the LORD Forever.

Psalm 23:4, 6

Know therefore that the Lord your God is God; he is the faithful God, keeping his covenant of love to a thousand generations of those who love him and keep his commandments.

Deuteronomy 7:9 (NIV).

Remember your word to your servant, for you have given me hope. My comfort in my suffering is this: Your promise preserves my life.
Psalm 119:49-50 (NIV).

Because of the Lord's great love, we are not consumed, for his compassions never fail. They are new every morning; great is your faithfulness.
Lamentations 3:22-23 (NIV).

I will rejoice and be glad in your steadfast love, because you have seen my affliction; you have known the distress of my soul, and you have not delivered me into the hand of the enemy; you have set my feet in a broad place.
Psalm 31:7-8 (ESV)

For I am sure that neither death nor life, nor an- gels nor rulers, nor things present nor things to come, nor powers, nor height nor depth, nor any- thing else in all creation, will be able to separate us from the love of God in Christ Jesus our Lord.
Romans 8:38-39 (ESV).

www.ingramcontent.com/pod-product-compliance
Lightning Source LLC
LaVergne TN
LVHW041323080426
835513LV00008B/569